MW01241111

The You Scriptures

You are the One who You have been waiting for

10-2-10 gift

ISBN: 978-0-615-37429-1

10-4-10
Completed
1st real.

Cover Design and Book Design By: Lisa Corcoran

Divine Order
Right Actions....

June 2010 Print On Demand By:
Lightning Source, INC., USA
246 Heil Quaker Blvd.
La Vergne, TN 37086 USA

INNER
WORLD
PRESS

Inner World Press
P.O. Box 45911
Philadelphia PA 19149
www.innerworldpress.com

And now You will come to know who
You are not. To know in the eternal moment
that is always Now, that if Your Source be
for You, none are there left to be against
You.

Prayer of a New Beginning

In the name of the Eternal, of No-Beginning, of No-End. May Your journey of enlightenment be illuminated by Wisdom's guidance. May the recovery of Your Divinity banish chaos, fear, and misery from this place in the Universe forever. May Your True Self obliterate Your errors of mis-creation, the consequences of mis-thought, insuring Your safe arrival in the presence of the Beloved. And may the Hosts of the Eternal construct You a refuge of remembrance, so that this life represents the final occasion of Your descent into forgetfulness. And of Your blessings and prosperities, may they equal the number of grains of sand in all the face of the earth.

So it is that this prayer echoes throughout Eternity.

I. The Book of Your Coming Forth

BI. Ch.1:1-8

Infinite Wisdom

Life is eternal

Y ou may have heard this story, or You may have read these words in some version or another.

2   Yet in most recollections something is always amiss.

3   Many who knew the story firsthand could not write.

4   And so They depended on Those who could for the transmission thereof.

5   From word of mouth to paper the legend's magnitude became distorted.

6   Some were not conscious of the infallibility and the sheer intelligence of the Spirit that dwelled within it.

7   Others wanted merely to control the legend and You, honestly fearing that neither You nor the world were ready.

8   Enduring centuries of changing perspectives of Your true identity;

No beggining
No ending
Energy in motion

BI. Ch.1:9-13

9 Withstanding religions and the wars and conflicts
   surrounding them, the transmission and
   the legend were distorted even more.
10 But even before those times, Your coming forth
   bore responsibility for the avenue down which evil
   and temptation made their way into the world.
11 Some have maintained that these distortions are of no
   significance, that under no circumstances do they
   interfere with the plan.
12 They say You carry the memory within; that there
   are reminders in the phases of the moon, the arrival
   of the tides, and even in the most turbulent of storms.
13 They say You will hear it in the sweetest of music,
   feel it on summer nights as cool breezes chase away
   the day's heat.

BI. Ch.1:14-15

14 And that of a surety, the story will surface
    again, and again, and yet again.
15 You may not remember now, and You may
    never comprehend, the joy of Your coming forth
    from the No-Beginning, No-End.

BI. Ch.2:1-4

When there were as there are now, Beings who saw fit to do nothing more than light and adorn the Forever, a great event was witnessed throughout the Universes.

2   The coming forth of One graced with a small essence of Its Architect, the One who sculpts the Universes, blowing the brilliant breath of divine energy into them.

3   In the Worlds which have been identified and named, as well as in the Worlds in galaxies which remain unknown, You are a creation without precedent.

4   None had witnessed the blessing that would come to be known as You.

BI. Ch.2:5-8

5   None were there who could fathom how the Beloved
    could be more Generous, again sharing everything, but
    subtracting nothing from Itself.
6   Everyone gathered as if to see a great play, like waiting
    for the curtain to rise to see that which had been given
    the highest of accolades.
7   But this was a play of divine proportions of which
    You will find no earthly companion.
8   And the heavens have witnessed nothing like it since.

BI. Ch.3:1-5

When They communicated then as They do now, by vibration, Beings of the Universes circulated a joyful vibration throughout the Eternal.

2 It was an announcement of One to come forth with a destiny of divine magnitude.
3 One destined to possess a knowledge for which none of the Others were created, a knowledge surrounding a mystery of which the Others, in all the other Universes, knew not of.
4 This was to be a creation endowed with choice.
5 What could this possibly mean to Those who spend Their eternity reposed in the comfort of the Eternal's Presence, having not to make decisions, knowing nothing of choice?

BI. Ch.3:6-11

6   The Worlds marveled at Whom They would come to know as the Co-Creator in this Universe.
7   With faculties consisting solely of peace and gratitude.
8   They knew nothing of inquiry as such, knew of nothing to question.
9   They were as They are now: satisfied without self-consciousness.
10 Being an extension of Their Source, They feel nothing but a profound attraction which holds Them securely in the Eternal's embrace.
11 Endowed with the certainty of Generosity's magnificence, They continued as They always had and will, joyfully poised in the beauty of anticipatory tranquility.

BI. Ch.4:1-4

And it came to pass that out of the Eternal's unlimited abundance of ideas, Your forms were established, the body designed according to the ages and environs which You would choose to encounter.

2 Crafted with the precision of divine wholeness, directed by Its boundless Intelligence, You were unveiled before the Others.
3 How the High One created such a One as You still remains a mystery (to Them anyway).
4 This was a most beautiful, graceful, Co-Creating One as has been known throughout the Forever.

BI. Ch.4:5-10

5   Actually, none were there who knew the exact
    number of the inhabitants of the Universes, and there
    are none still.
6   But as They looked closer, without the assistance
    of eyes, and with nothing to express words, They
    released a joyful vibration of weeping throughout
    Eternity.
7   And into the far reaches of the Forever, the sound
    of adoration and wonder still travels.
8   Just a symphony of joyful weeping which
    instruments could never, to the end of Eternity,
    replicate.
9   Weeping.
10 But no tears.

BI. Ch.5:1-4

Under Wisdom's guidance, Heaven's Inhabitants witnessed divine thought's vibration slowing, nestling Itself within the crystals of a divine extension.

2 You, a World created to experience time and space, a World created to transcend them both.

3 A World with a Mind capable of creating like unto Itself, having no model from which to work.

4 A World capable of experiencing emotions which were heretofore unknown throughout the Forever.

BI. Ch.5:5-8

5 A World whose beauty lies in Its chosen
   destiny, to come forth safeguarding and expressing
   the desires of Its Beloved, Its Source of All That Is.
6 This was a World endowed with knowledge of Itself.
7 And yet a World that had to learn that a World It was.
8 The Others, still not quite sure of the implications of
   Your coming forth, only took all this to mean yet
   another expression of the Eternal's Beneficence.

BI. Ch.6:1-4

Now amid the usual joy and jubilation, They witnessed as the No-Beginning, No-End blew the energy that quickens and enlivens into You.

2 The same energy responsible for the constant flaming of the suns.

3 Disks of the most brilliant hues were placed in back of You, along with a fire that warms and informs them.

4 And above You, a closed flower of celestial brilliance, poised to expose its luminosity at Your decision to acknowledge Your Source and return to It.

BI. Ch. 6:5-8

5   The Worlds witnessed as Wisdom gave You the
knowledge of Yourself, as It informed You of the
responsibilities of Your coming forth:

6   "Be like the Others," were Its words, "reposed
in peace and tranquility, or spend part of Your
Eternity experiencing Yourself, taking on a myriad
of forms in places of which You choose, of which
You create."

7   The Worlds, knowing nothing of *responsibility,*
trusted Wisdom as It translated into a vibration
of which They could know.

8   "For the journey, It has been given the
knowledge of Itself and the *desire* to return.

BI. Ch.6:9-11

9   But It must travel into the far recesses of Itself,
Its mind, beyond the crowded pathways of what will
certainly become a burdensome forgetfulness.
10 There It will find that knowing Itself is knowing
the way back."
11 The Others, seemingly assured of Your safety,
are presently awaiting Your return.

BI. Ch.7:1-6

S ome say it was an explosion.

2   Others deny it emphatically, constantly
    recalculating the years based on this or that
    piece of new evidence.
3   Experts say You were 65 million years in
    the evolving.
4   Some are saying seven days which is equal,
    Their books say, to the blink of an eye.
5   Many remain silent, seeing no benefit in the
    speculation thereof.
6   Then there are Those who were present and
    who know not how to forget.

BI. Ch.7:7-11

7   They know exactly what transpired and that it could not
    have occurred within the limitations of time and space.
8   Of those half say They heard a faint whisper,
    felt as the heavens were plunged into a deafening
    silence, then a blinding brilliance of light.
9   They say, though, that there are some things
    which are of a surety, and on which You can rely:
10 The Eternal placed within You Your Origin, the
    Knowledge of It, and the desire to be conscious of It.
11 You can ignore it for a time, but it can never be
    silenced.

End of BookI

II. The Book of Your Journey

BII. Ch.1:1-5

S peak now from the depths of Your being, the truth of who You are, from where You come, and who You represent.

2 You are an extension of the Source, the Perpetually Self-Creating One, the No-Beginning, No-End.

3 The energy that is You is undying, forever transforming, always expanding, always was, and always will be.

4 There has never been a time that it was not, no space has it ever not occupied.

5 It knows of that which is hidden and the origin of everything seen.

BII. Ch.1:6-9

6 Of goodness' passion lying within the depths of
   the heart, the fertile passion of ideas, some forgotten,
   most hidden.

7 This energy is the same in quality (although not
   quantity) as Your Origin.

8 It knows for certain that You have been here
   many times, having simply changed eras and
   locales.

9 The certain knowledge of Your journeying and the
   experiences thereof are known only in Its Presence,
   the One Who shares everything with You.

BII. Ch.1:10-12

10 But now, in this era, in the circumstances and situations in which You live, Your eternal identity awaits revelation.

11 You are like a mirror, reflecting the Forever.

12 When You gaze inward, You gaze towards Eternity.

BII. Ch.2:1-4

Have You never taken notice of the energy contained in a flower seed, as it too has journeyed out of Eternity, its Infinite Source.

2 You and the energy contained in the seed share the same Origin.

3 You do not know the stops it has made, where the expressions took place, but that it now chooses to absorb the experiences of light, water and nutrients from the earth.

4 It is the Eternal's commanding and directing of the energy which creates the seed and the flower's form, which, despite appearances, admits no repetition, no sameness.

BII. Ch.2:5-9

5   A faint knowledge of this creative ability is
    with You, but the divine method for demonstrating
    it has been eclipsed.
6   Maybe Your wandering has caused You to forget.
7   Maybe the attractions and experiences from the places
    of Your wandering have pushed the memory farther and
    farther into abandonment and misuse.
8   But this is the journey in which Your abilities and the
    divine method for their realization are revealed.
9   This journey removes the veil from Your true
    identity.

BII. Ch.2:10

10 This is the journey for which You will shine
forth as the Co-Creator, commanding energy,
calling forth physical demonstrations of spiritual
realities.

BII. Ch.3:1-4

Listen, the energy residing in the seed knows its destiny: expansion.

2   It is not slowed down nor hindered by the illusion of choosing, nor is it distracted by circumstances or concerns about the profits it will garner.

3   It does not engage in conflicts with its Source, nor does it shun the guidance of It.

4   Its journey is one of non-resistance, and when its season as flower is complete, it will appear, to You, to die.

BII. Ch.3:5-8

5   But make no mistake; energy simply expands
    out of form, signaling its continuation on its journey.
6   Its expansion is eternal, no one but the Caretaker
    of energy knowing how many forms it will take.
7   This is one of the many processes which serve
    as a sign and reminder about Your relationship
    with the No-Beginning, No-End.
8   Know the joy that lies in such intimacy with
    the Eternal.

BII. Ch.4:1-5

The energy which expresses Itself as seed and flower is a fraction of the energy which resides in You.

2   Your journey is one of learning to command this energy, which requires little or no physical strain on Your part.

3   But it does require that You awaken to a living, breathing consciousness of who You are.

4   Every lesson about creating is a lesson about You.

5   Each lesson establishes a stronger bond of attraction between You and Your Origin, drawing You closer and closer to Your Self.

BII. Ch.4:6-9

6 In You resides the ideas, without repetition,
   for the expression of this energy, as creating is
   part and parcel of Your nature.
7 This part of Your experience is one of joy,
   a joy that will be in exact measure to Your
   willingness to express Your Origin's Will and
   Desires for You.
8 You have already fulfilled the prerequisites
   for this task: You asked to come here to remember,
   to do so in physical manifestation, a body form.
9 Prepared and outfitted, You are a Co-Creator
   with an immense responsibility.

BII. Ch.4:10-11

10 And while Your travels bear much responsibility for Your forgetfulness, this earthly sojourn bears the responsibility for far more.

11 For it is here that You will experience a substantial shift in Your reality, where You ascend from existing in the physical, to consciously living in the Eternal Stream of Goodness from which You originated.

BII. Ch.5:1-4

You carry with You the sum total of experiences that You have assimilated since Your departure from the No-Beginning, No-End.

2 And it is here that You will contribute and share Your legacy of experiences for the prosperity and well-being of Those with whom You share the Eternal.

3 The knowledge from these experiences will form the basis of Your next manifestation, in form and locale, if You so choose.

4 But, in any case, here You will have learned how to conduct Yourself as a citizen of the Universe.

BII. Ch.5:5-8

5 You are on a journey of experiences, a journey of discovery, where the identity which some sought to suppress is laid bear for All to witness.

6 A journey of recovery, where the responsibilities which You were informed of at Your coming forth, are accepted anew, in the Presence of Your Eternal.

7 A journey of restoration, where the awakening to Your true identity will help restore sanity to a fraction of a Universe plunged into the depths of madness.

8 A madness, however small, which is destabilizing the earth.

BII. Ch.5:9-11

9   And without this sacred space, the energy that
    is You loses one of the most conducive
    environments by which to awaken to Itself.

10 Your life and Your energy are one, and Your
    energy and the energy of the Universe are inseparable.

11 The decisions You make determine the quality
    and direction of Your life, contributing to and
    influencing the decisions of Those with Whom
    You share the Presence of the Eternal.

BII. Ch.6:1-5

Your life's transactions on earth are governed by the choices You make.

2 It is a divine governance, differing in form
   and essence from the manner in which Your life as
   a citizen on earth is controlled.
3 Now You may look around You, noting sadness,
   despair and utter chaos, and wonder how
   a divine self-governance is possible.
4 The question is not how can You express Your
   divinity under the circumstances in which You live.
5 But rather, how will those circumstances
   continue to exist under the glaring reality of Your
   divinity?

BII. Ch.6:6-9

6 Divine responsibility, deliberate and conscious choosing, deliberate and conscious creation, deliberate and conscious intent.

7 The world You once knew will give way for the new.

8 Here, You will practice making choices about what You do with Your energy.

9 But know that real living will begin when You remember that <u>You joyfully</u> placed choosing under <u>the guidance</u> of Your Self, the No-Beginning, No-End.

BII. Ch.6:10-12

10 Understand the abilities which are at
     your command.
11 You must learn the rules first in order to use
     them effectively and consciously for the prosperity
     of the Universe, for the prosperity of Yourself.
12 You must learn the rules in order to get the
     most joy and happiness out of Your journey here.

BII. Ch.7:1-4

Know that Your choices are Your responsibility,
and no one has control over Your divine right,
  unless You choose to give that responsibility away.

2 It is the ability to consciously make choices,
   to consciously create which will deliver You to
   the Presence of Your Origin where freedom
   and security reside.
3 Otherwise, You mis-create (mis-directed energy
   with faulty purpose).
4 Maybe You remember from time to time, having
   a faint vision of previous experiences and places,
   other forms You have taken.

BII. Ch.7:5-9

5 It is better for You that You ask for no
   interpretations.

6 You must be the expert in You now.

7 A conscious return is a conscious recognition
   of Your divinity, Your sacred identity.

8 Your journeying, the number of Your experiences
   outside Your Origin, no one knows for certain,
   except for the Eternal.

9 And none are there who can interpret Your
   realities without casting onto them, some
   interpretation which bears no resemblance to
   Your experiences.

BII. Ch.7:10-12

10 Innumerable are the Ones journeying, each with
     a path, designed by the same Architect, destined
     for the same Origin.
11 Inexplicable and indefinable is the One in the
     Many, the multiple expressions of the One, Eternal,
     of No-Beginning, No-End.
12 It is incomprehensible that You could have consciously
     chosen to forget what You will make one of Your life's
     goals to remember.

End of BookII

III. The Book of Wisdom

BIII. Ch.1:1-7

Many have spoken of the beauty and magnificence of Wisdom.

2 To apply its teachings is to practice being in the presence of Your Origin.
3 Know that many find Wisdom far easier to talk about than to practice.
4 It is Wisdom's role to alert You to insincerity.
5 It is with You to dispel the grandest illusions, the most well thought out deceptions.
6 It opens doors which You have closed, smoothes the paths You riddle with obstacles.
7 Wisdom restores light where You have recklessly summoned darkness.

BIII. Ch.1:8-11

8 It urges You to change Your mind often to facilitate growth and expansion.

9 For next to impossible is it to change Your life, without changing the way You think about It and Yourself.

10 Wisdom informs Your will of its true nature, and without Its guidance, You run the risk of using your abilities dangerously.

11 You cause misery and suffering, when within You resides the talent to bless and heal.

BIII. Ch.2:1-4

Listen. Some have said that in Your journeying, You will encounter 10,000 illusions whose responsibility it is to make sure You never discover Your true identity.

2 Those illusions exist solely to prevent the knowledge of who You are from reaching You.

3 Although 10,000 in number, the essence of their messages can be summed up accordingly: you are a physical being, and there is nothing about you which suggests a divine origin.

4 Wisdom is Your protection and guide in moving beyond these messages.

BIII. Ch.2:5-7

5 It transfers knowledge to You in such a way
   that these delusions will dissolve and not become
   a hindrance to Your journey.
6 Knowing all languages and being an expert in
   the language of madness, Wisdom will transfer the
   true knowledge of Your identity to You.
7 In the face of the world's denial, which will
   ultimately lead to its disappearance, Wisdom will
   gently convince You that the knowledge of
   who You are has always been with You.

BIII. Ch.2:8

8 And to insure that Your journey of transformation and recovery is one of joy and peace is Wisdom's responsibility and Your purpose.

BIII. Ch.3:1-4

You can begin to reclaim Your identity from the experiences that You have here, but know that Wisdom's guidance must be requested.

2   Given the responsibility to host Your journey, Wisdom cannot impose Its assistance.

3   But once You call on It, the Eternal will ensure Its arrival, overseeing It as It shields You from misinformation, barring any guidance which does not serve Your journey.

4   You see, Wisdom is a translator, knowing where You come from, knowing where You are now.

BIII. Ch.3:5-8

5 It translates from Its place in the
   No-Beginning, No-End to Its place in You.
6 Wisdom never left Its Origin, yet It is able
   to journey with You.
7 It hears Your questions, is informed of Your
   desires, but, most importantly, It will guide You
   through an understanding of Your abilities,
   Your successes, Your resistance.
8 It is under Wisdom's guidance that You will
   become conscious of how You use Your share
   of divine inheritance—this intelligent energy.

BIII. Ch.3:9-10

9 Under Wisdom's guidance You will know whether
   or not Your choices are reflecting Your Origin's
   Will or the unconscionable desires of the world in
   which You are a temporary inhabitant.
10 And even in the discernment of Your Beloved's
    Will from the world's (or the ego's) baseless
    needs, You will confront and dispel those 10,000
    illusions.

BIII. Ch.4:1-5

There is no difficulty in answering questions, none in fulfilling desires, no tentativeness in responses.

2   All questions are answered, all desires fulfilled,
    but Wisdom knows that often You are not yet aware that
    what You seek is that which is seeking You;
    not conscious that everything for which You
    have asked has been given.

3   As You begin to remember what You consciously
    ask, You will begin to recognize the immediacy of
    Wisdom's responses.

4   Wisdom does not experience distractions or
    disappointments.

5   It is not fatigued by the amount of time that it is
    taking You to look within.

BIII. Ch.4:6-10

6 It is not governed by choice and knows nothing
   of it.
7 It only knows that It must reveal events and
   circumstances that are orchestrated for You,
   at a time chosen by Your Self.
8 It is in these events and circumstances that
   You will find the signs that signal Your closeness
   to Your Origin, to recovering Your true identity.
9 Wisdom could communicate with You directly,
   which would increase the speed of Your journeying.
10 But direct communication requires solitude and
   the lack of fear to hear the Voice that most certainly
   dwells within.

BIII. Ch.5:1-6

M any are the lessons You will learn from Wisdom:

2   That it is inseparable from You, actually residing
    in Your Origin, having been there at Your coming forth.
3   Residing in that place, the same place You are
    destined, It guides, translates, and transfers.
4   It regulates and knows the exact number of Your
    waking hours, and of Your sleep.
5   It has calculated with precision the number of
    breaths You will require.
6   It knows the details of every form You want to
    take.

BIII. Ch.5:7-10

7 It recognizes and understands the workings of the 10,000 illusions.

8 It knows of Your innermost and sincere longing to return Your Heart to its rightful Owner, the No-Beginning, No-End.

9 The Eternal.

10 The Most Beloved.

BIII. Ch.6:1-5

Wisdom is one of Your Origin's greatest gifts.

2 It is a great teacher, teaching that what You
see on the outside is the essence of the beliefs You
carry within.
3 Your life here is inspired.
4 It is here that Wisdom will inform You, again,
about the relationship between Your physical life
and Your spiritual life until the distinction
dissolves.
5 Your life here is with eternal purpose.

BIII. Ch.6:6-11

6 You will come to know that thoughts which go on
   within (despite their lack of verbal expression)
   will produce form at some level.

7 There will be no surprises in any of the
   circumstances which unfold in Your life.

8 Your life here is miraculous.

9 With this gift of Wisdom, You determine Your
   distance from the Origin.

10 You determine Your closeness to the Presence
   of the No-Beginning, No-End, Eternal One.

11 You will come to know that for Your sake, there
   is nothing that the Beloved has not thought of.

BIII. Ch.7:1-5

Y ou choose the tempo of Your traveling.

2   This traveling, this journeying is the
    awakening process to Your livingness in the
    Eternal, the Now.
3   Every lesson learned, every question answered,
    every desire fulfilled is but a summoning of
    energy, which contains within it the medium for
    drawing You closer and closer to home.
4   Wisdom only guides to fruition that which is
    aligned with Its Origin.
5   But You can guide, without It and with much
    effort, situations and circumstances which will push
    You farther and farther away, in awareness (not fact),
    from Your Source.

BIII. Ch.7:6-9

6　And without Wisdom's guidance, You will only usher in sadness and misery.

7　Learn to commune with It regularly, meeting It frequently in the gardens of silence and ~~tranquility~~.

8　Listen as It reminds You of Yourself.

9　Trust ~~It as It informs~~ You of Your Eternalness.

End of BookIII

IV. The Book of Responsibilities

BIV. Ch.1:1-5

Your Self knows, but You have chosen to forget.

2   Choose to remember now that of the many
    responsibilities You have, there are seven of
    prime importance.
3   It is by their knowledge that You were created
    and by them that Your journey is governed, whether
    it will be marked by success or resistance.
4   It is by the knowledge of them that You will
    reduce the time it takes You to pass through here,
    returning to Your Origin.
5   It is by them that You will become known as
    the blessing and prosperity of the Worlds.

BIV. Ch.1:6-7

6 It is by them that You create, and it is
   without them that You will indeed experience
   resistance and setbacks.
7 And it is by this knowing that You have
   fulfilled the first responsibility.

BIV. Ch.2:1-4

In You resides the truth of the No-Beginning, No-End, the fact that It always was and always will be.

2   By it You know of Your own Eternalness that is Your true Self.

3   In it You will find refuge from the fear of death, destruction, and misfortune, knowing that only the continuation of well being flows from It.

4   Your awakening makes plain to You that life is not only spiritual, but that it flows into an ocean of joy, wealth, and vibrant health.

BIV. Ch.2:5-7

5 In It You are liberated from anxiety, freed
   from preoccupations about conditions and
   circumstances over which You have no control.
6 And in the Eternal, You fully experience the
   happiness and joy that is in Reality, Now.
7 It is the responsibility of knowing the Eternal
   Who resides in You that You witness some of the
   divine splendor of the All That Is.

BIV. Ch.3:1-7

S top and take notice of all that surrounds You.

2 It is all changing and will eventually pass
   away.
3 Everything passes away except for the
   No-Beginning, No-End, Eternal.
4 Change can be witnessed and understood as
   energy manifests in forms and then withdraws, over
   and over and over again.
5 You cannot find a place where change is not.
6 This changing insures Your attachment to no
   form.
7 It insures that You only seek closeness with
   the Source and Director of that change, the Eternal.

BIV. Ch.3:7-10

8   This is the way the Beloved operates in
    manifestation, energy taking up no permanent
    habitation, no permanent abode.
9   You know not sometimes nor understand that
    which the Eternal gives life to, the chosen
    expressions of Itself.
10 But You can know for sure that energy is
    Intelligently directed by the Eternal Presence,
    the All That Is.

BIV. Ch.4:1-4

Thought is energy, and You are energy, being a Divine thought of the No-Beginning, No-End.

2 You would do well not to engage in disputes about Your true nature, for the responsibility of the definition of You is Yours.

3 You discover the nature of Your Mind, the nature of Your thoughts, for it is by them that You will summon and command energy, shaping and molding it however You desire.

4 This is the manner in which the Origin unites ideas with energy, and this is the manner in which the Origin operates in You and through You.

BIV. Ch.4:5-8

5 Since energy is of the Eternal, there is no
   reality to scarcity, for only eternal abundance
   and well being ensue from this Source.
6 And the ideas of lack and limitation have no
   witnesses in the presence of the Eternal.
7 As You master this responsibility, You claim
   ownership of Your divinity.
8 As You claim ownership of Your divinity, You
   will begin to experience life as Co-Creator.

BIV. Ch.5:1-5

You have heard because much has been said about the *Law of Attraction.*

2 It is Your responsibility not only to know it, but to cooperate with it.

3 By it, You are expanding the Universe of which You are an extension.

4 When You become conscious of Your creative abilities, You will only bring into manifestation that which is characteristic of Your Source, the No-Beginning, No-End.

5 Once You have settled on Your creation, it is imperative that You nurture it by joyfully preparing for its appearance.

BIV. Ch.5:6-10

6 In this process, You are witnessing Your
   Divine nature, a testament and affirmation of who
   You are;
7 And reaffirmation that the creative elixir
   —expectation, belief, and faith—form the basis
   for bringing into physical manifestation, ideas
   from on high.
8 This is the energy that gives birth to galaxies.
9 This is the energy You use to transform conditions.
10 If You become consciously aware of knowing
   that by thought, You can summon anything into Your
   life, You quickly recognize the power in thought.

BIV. Ch.5:11-16

11 Most importantly, You will discover the
    illusion of *freedom* where choice is concerned.

12 With the Law of Attraction, You will see how
    it is impossible to choose to bring into life that
    which has no affinity with Your thought.

13 In other words, You will attract into Your life
    only events and circumstances for which You have
    prepared the mental groundwork.

14 Allow the stream of well being and goodness to
    guide thought.

15 This is how the law works.

16 In this matter, there is no other choice.

BIV. Ch.6:1-5

Know that You have traveled divinely and graciously into this world and just as graciously, You will exit.

2   You can lighten this journey by laying aside some of the world's advice thereof.
3   Therefore, reconsider the belief in both sin and hell, for many have created suffering in this life because of this belief.
4   The belief in sin and hell instills fear and guilt, creating a barrier to the entry of joy and happiness.
5   The belief in sin and hell do little, but mostly nothing, to strengthen Your relationship with Your Origin.

BIV. Ch.6:6-9

6 Even in the world in which You live, the
   prospect of hell has not served as a deterrent
   to anything.

7 In fact it only makes for a deep-seated
   dislike and fear for an imagined, jealous deity
   whose ego is easily offended by *his* creations,
   whom he has complete control over.

8 Who adores and seeks union with one who
   threatens its creations with the torment of burning
   flesh?

9 As You draw closer to Your Origin, You will
   know that a mistake can be corrected.

BIV. Ch.6:10-13

10 That offenses are of Your unconscious defining.
11 Know that the Divine cannot be insulted or offended,
   made angry or sad by anything that You are capable of.
12 The world in which You live is totally
   incapable of confronting errors which originate
   in thought (this being the only possible origin of
   error).
13 It only seeks solutions which are punishing
   rather than corrective in nature, seeking always
   some discomfort or harm to the body.

BIV. Ch.6:13-18

14 In some cases, it seeks to destroy it (the body)
    as punishment, not understanding that that which
    produced it is Eternal.
15 The mythology of hell is mis-creation, a
    product of mis-thought.
16 But far more insane is it to believe in a
    distance or separation between You and Your Origin.
17 Depriving Yourself of the comfort of Its
    Presence because You believe that It harbors anger
    and rancor.
18 This insane reasoning and the conflict it
    produces is about as close as You can arrive
    at the world's imaginings of hell.

BIV. Ch.7:1-4

In the environment of insanity (that this world is), the need to judge and be judged carries with it significant barriers to the realization of Your true identity.

2   The responsibility to eliminate the need to judge and be judged carries with it the responsibility to accept on face value, that beyond all forms, beyond all appearances, lies the Presence of the Eternal.

3   *No exceptions*

4   In judging, You first bear witness against Yourself for failing to recognize the unassailability of Omniscience (of which You are an extension).

BIV. Ch.7:5-8

5 You have yet to understand that judgment,
   good or bad, is recognized and valued within
   before it is projected without.

6 All You will ever be able to do is demonstrate
   that You are of a <u>unified Eternalness that has no</u>
   <u>outside for You to be, or to judge *from*</u>.

7 As an Aspect of the Source, You only have access to
   <u>Your Self, which in fact is Everything</u>.

8 And it is only from the unawakened part of You,
   that part which awaits Your claim of ownership,
   that judgment is not only possible, but totally
   acceptable.

BIV. Ch.7:9-12

9   In the light of Wisdom, the Eternal pervades
    all, Its Presence total, despite the illusion of
    appearances.
10 Finally, the need to be judged stems from an
    unyielding misconception that validation of Your
    Being could possibly come from a world poised to
    destroy You if You oppose it.
11 In the relinquishment of judgment, a powerful
    discernment is acquired.
12 You, who up until now provided support for
    an insane way of living, have relinquished all
    investment in judgment.

BIV. Ch.7:13-15

13 When You peacefully withdraw support, You make
    a small, but significant contribution to dismantling
    an erroneous way of living.
14 You make a huge contribution and set the example,
    regardless of the world's *judgement,* for the possibility
    of living life in new ways.
15 Devoid of judgment.

End of BookIV

V. The Book of Love

BV. Ch.1:1-7

Many You have heard say that It is a thing uncreated.

2 Some say that like Your Eternal, It was, is and always will be.
3 For certain You can rely on Its workings in all situations and in all circumstances.
4 Know that It obeys the One who knows Its true nature and who speaks the truth about It.
5 Its nature is that of kindness and generosity.
6 It knows not of discord or grievance, strife nor violence.
7 It is fond of peace and is the main ingredient of joy.

BV. Ch.1:8-9

8   It is responsible for the grandest passion in
    the Forever.
9   It is the uncontestable affection the Eternal
    has for Itself.

BV. Ch.2:1-6

Many You have heard say It is a thing synonymous with Its Origin, that They are One.

2   Of a surety, It dissolves the most hardened conditions, solves problems of the grandest magnitude.

3   It is the first to respond to Your pleas for help, Your desire for relief, for peace.

4   You can no more ignore It than You can the inevitable awakening that stirs within Your depths.

5   By It great healings take place, miracles witnessed.

6   Under Its direction, sadness and misery are transformed into joy and peace.

BV. Ch.2:7

7   The earth would spin out of control without Its
    tutelage.

BV. Ch.3:1-4

Many You have heard say It is the reason by which You came forth, that It informed the thought that is You.

2 Maybe, but for sure It delivered You safely to this destination, and It will deliver You safely to the next.

3 You cannot live without It anymore than You can live without the breath of the Eternal which flows through You.

4 Without It, the awakening and transformation for which You journey would be impossible; for It is the attraction by which You draw closer to Your Origin.

BV. Ch.3:5-6

5 It is because of It that You overlook the
   accusations and insults of the Unawakened, knowing
   that in Love They know not what They think, what
   They say or do.
6 By the company of It, night and day enjoy a
   peaceful partnership, no conflict, no competition.

BV. Ch.4:1-5

Many You have heard say It is You from head to toe.

2   That every single cell of Your physical body is
    based in It.
3   That Your very creations ride into manifestation
    on Its breath.
4   For certain, You can know that the Worlds would
    not exist had it not been for Its willingness to give
    everything of Itself.
5   By It, even the illusion of the separation of Your
    physical world and spiritual world is kept in a
    safe, perfect balance until You are ready to know
    otherwise.

BV. Ch.4:6-7

6 It orchestrates the inhalation and exhalation
   of the breath.
7 It is because of It that Wisdom hosts Your
   journey.

BV. Ch.5:1-7

Y ou have undoubtedly heard it said that It has an opposite, that everything does.

2   This is only the opinion of those unfamiliar with it.
3   In the Eternal, there is no opposition.
4   And there is no opposition to Love.
5   It is informed of everything, but knows not of a rival.
6   In the stream of well-being, nothing is there to challenge the recognition of worthiness that flows from the Eternal through You and to You.
7   That is Love.

BV. Ch.5:8-10

8 Before Love, You witness the dissolution of
   suffering and misery—both unable to resist Love's
   attraction.
9 From Love, You can witness a joy for which You
   have no words to describe.
10 And with it, in the blink of an eye, You will
    traverse a thousand years on Your return journey.

BV. Ch.6:1-5

Y ou see through Its vision how everything changes.

2 That what was once perplexing is now
   experienced with perfect clarity.
3 That what was once a source of anxiety has been
   replaced by a refuge of solace and consolation.
4 That what was once a source of depression is
   replaced by what is now reassurance that life is
   not only good, but also Eternal.
5 That Your inability to find a stable center
   (if You thought of finding one at all), is now
   replaced by a light-filled path leading to Your
   Origin.

BV. Ch.6:6-7

6 That the thought of Your lack is now replaced
   by the certain knowledge of *You are love; You are
   abundance.*
7 That the once empty places within You are now
   filled with the evidence of Love's existence.

BV. Ch.7:1-5

What can You think of that Love could not possibly respond to?

2 Because of It, all the Universes have an equal share in the Eternal.

3 It is because of It that You can rely on the knowing of the heart to get You through just about anything.

4 Under Its direction, You *will* the command that mountains be moved, and the No-Beginning, No-End withdraws Its energy, and they make haste to another place.

5 Under Its guidance, time collapses and space dissolves.

BV. Ch.7:6-7

6   By It Your safety is guaranteed, and obstacles retreat, bowing down in salutation as You pass by at the speed of light.
7   By It, the Worlds, poised in tranquility, await Your return.

End of BookV

VI. The Book of Obstacles

BVI. Ch.1:1-5

The awakening brings relief from constriction, ushering in an expanded vision of who You truly are.

2   It ushers in a joy and peace which indeed surpasses understanding.
3   Your willingness to remember and Your yearning to know the Presence in which You live, breathe and have Your being is a call for which Wisdom responds.
4   No doubt, ease accompanies the recovery of Your inheritance.
5   And no doubt You are aware of the jubilation of the Heavens, who are rejoicing that Your awakening is on the horizon.

BVI. Ch.1:6-10

6 Now is the time to clear a few lingering
   obstacles from Your path.
7 With another step forward, resistance retreats.
8 The time between the idea's inspiration and its
   manifestation decreases.
9 Your happiness is more stable, and peace's presence
   more reliable.
10 It's just a few ideas which may have lingered,
   ideas which must be reckoned with in Wisdom's
   light and Love's mercy.

BVI. Ch.2:1-4

You once believed that You were a victim of circumstance, that Your life was created from without, that woe was You.

2   So the thought of who would direct You and to where was a question You asked of the world in which You live.

3   While it is true that You live life in the physical, it must be clear to You now that You and circumstances are under the clear direction of the larger, unseen part of You.

4   Your awakening makes plain to You that life is not only spiritual, but that it flows into an ocean of joy, wealth, and vibrant health.

BVI. Ch.2:5-6

5 Even Your physical body is nothing more than
Spirit's Love vibrating at a visible rate.
6 Now You turn towards the Origin, to Whom You
can rely on and trust.

BVI. Ch.3:1-6

Y ou once believed in lack and scarcity.

2 *You* created the belief that You must somehow
   go without.
3 The belief that suffering must accompany life
   (and progress) must be held up to the light of
   Wisdom.
4 For some say that the belief in suffering gave
   rise to the belief in lack and scarcity.
5 Suffering only accompanies the insanity which
   attends unconsciousness.
6 Suffering is believing that You can somehow be
   in a state of disconnectedness from that which
   gives You life.

BVI. Ch.3:7-10

7   Releasing erroneous beliefs will place You
    closer to Your Original state of peace.

8   It is a release which produces, in moments,
    knowledge that will take You thousands of years to
    figure out if You continue to believe that suffering
    is a part of life.

9   It is the knowledge of Your true nature, well-being,
    which the energy is attracted to, which expands,
    constantly yielding a new version of You.

10 It is the knowledge that *in the moment*
    beyond the awakening, You can experience
    Your Self in an infinite number of ways.

BVI. Ch.3:11-12

11 It is the knowledge that out of Love You were created of abundance and that You never were and never will be without.

12 Surely You must see now that the belief You held in lack and scarcity is what surely invited them both into Your life.

BVI. Ch.4:1-6

You remember how You once believed that if there was a heaven, that it most certainly was outside and above You?

2   Wisdom has now assured You that the state of peace of which You are becoming accustomed, the safety You feel in the presence of Your Origin is real.

3   And that although You were taught that heaven comes after life, no doubt You know now that heaven is here.

4   Heaven is now.

5   Heaven is within.

6   Heaven is that peace.

BVI. Ch.4:7-12

7   And heaven expands whenever You express Love
    and gratitude for It.

8   You are heaven's architect.

9   Now understanding Your place in the Universe,
    You can respond in the ways of Your Origin:
    blessing without reservation; loving without limits.

10 Now You build cosmic mansions within, rooms
    furnished with the décor of Eternity.

11 The cool breezes of Wisdom's certainty replace
    the unsettling and destructive winds of ignorance.

12 Your prayers become ones of gratitude, and Your
    need becomes only to draw closer to Your Self.

BVI. Ch.5:1-4

You once believed that there were buildings in the world which represented Your Origin, which claimed authority on Its word.

2 Now, You witness a multitude of Hosts who, outside those buildings, point the way to the next step forward.

3 Withdrawing some of the Energy that You once placed in beliefs in the words of bygone days allows fresh revelations of Now to inform and inspire You.

4 And You will know that the truth You thought before the awakening will look and feel dramatically different from the truth You think after the awakening.

BVI. Ch.5:5-6

5   In this manner, Your Divinity becomes more in
    focus, in the present, not frozen in a past
    that never was, or in a future that will never be.
6   Wisdom will continue to remind You of living
    in the present until You discontinue looking back
    for guidance and definitions of Yourself in the
    world's past.

BVI. Ch.6:1-5

You once believed that You were ushered into this
life by darkness and shame.

2   Now as You begin to peer within, You cannot
find their dwelling place.
3   Unhesitating, You now look within and there
abounds only dwellings overflowing with the lights
of certitude.
4   Indeed there is just no place now for darkness
and shame to hide.
5   You will begin to look within more frequently.

BVI. Ch.6:6-7

6   Know that the time will come when Your vision
    of Your inner world will be indistinguishable from
    Your vision of Your outer world.
7   And in love and gratitude, You will wonder how
    it ever was that You wasted some of Your Eternal
    Now looking for Your Self outside of *You*.

BVI. Ch.7:1-6

You will come to know that what You once believed
is no longer important for Your journey into the moment
that is always now.

2 Those beliefs serve only as a witness to the
distance You have traveled.
3 You will visit them from time to time, but less
and less frequently, until You will forget You
once knew them at all.
4 Now, joy-filled remembering of Your Origin
requires every breath You take.
5 With their misinformed mythologies having been
dismantled and gently laid aside, the voices from
the places where Your old beliefs took You become
fainter and fainter.
6 Sacrifice is no longer necessary, suffering just a
clear misguided philosophy above how to live.

BVI. Ch.7:7-10

7   Now, without leaving Your Origin, You craft a
    blessing guided by Wisdom and informed by Love.
8   From Your consciousness as Co-Creator, these
    obstacles are now removed.
9   And another door to degradation, falsehood,
    and misery sealed.
10 *Shut.*

End of BookVI

VII. The Book of Eternal Continuation

BVII. Ch.1:1-7

Now You are drawing near to the path of eternal expansion.

2   This is the way, one that is in alignment with Your purpose.

3   No Host could have made this decision for You.

4   None are there in the Forever Who have power over Your will.

5   And none are there Who have the authority to override the law which finds expression in You and through You.

6   You now have only to understand the magnitude of Your choice.

7   And know that this is not the first time that You have come thus far.

BVII. Ch.1:8-11

8   But Those in the Heavens pray that this time
     will be Your last.
9   The ways of life lived in the world are tiring.
10 The ways of life lived in the Presence of the
     Eternal are infinitely joyous.
11 To see and know the difference *is* the awakening.

BVII. Ch.2:1-6

D o You want to exist in a world which knows not of who You are?

2 A world that likens You to your name, your color, your sex, and the biggest insult of all, to what you eat?

3 This is the world which offers the gifts of uncertainty, worry, and fatigue.

4 This is the world which is concerned not of the gifts which You can contribute.

5 But of how much of you can be consumed for no other purpose than greed.

6 This is the world which will offer you everything.

BVII. Ch.2:7-11

7 Within limits.

8 And again you will be outraged after you realize you get nothing.

9 This is the world which knows not of You nor of Your Source.

10 And only in its arrogance does it claim to be Your Origin.

11 The world cannot acknowledge the Eternal, for surely that would signal the end of its tyrannical reign.

BVII. Ch.3:1-5

O f this world there is little to look forward to.

2   After a while, You will seek to dull the pain
    that certainly comes from ignoring Your Self,
    from ignoring that burning desire to seek union
    with You.

3   You will seek relief from the transitory nature of
    the world, not knowing that there is no refuge from
    it except down the path created *for* You.

4   The world will tell You that something is amiss, that
    maybe You have problems.

5   When in fact, You came into the world to restore
    it to sanity, to make this earth reflect the heaven it was
    before You forgot Your purpose.

BVII. Ch.3:6-9

6 And You, who will never grow small enough to fit into this world, will be kept from the awareness of the presence of Your Eternal because You listen to those who know You not.

7 Certainly You must see that the beliefs You hold about Your Self speak lies to the reality of who You truly are.

8 Here is where You realize that You must remember Your Origin, that the only real choice is for a return to the presence of the No-Beginning, No-End, Eternal One.

9 Here, in this moment, You can choose between littleness and constraint, or nobility and eternal expansion.

BVII. Ch.4:1-5

Down the path created for You, You will find everything for which to realize Your divinity.

2   On the path back to Your Origin, time will expand, allowing You to have experiences which expand Your sense of joy and happiness.

3   The abundance for which You were created, and the abundance of which You were created will only attract more to You.

4   The journey back home will be one of appreciation and gratitude for which You will enjoy almost as much as the joy of the journey's goal:

5   To realize that You and Your Self are the same, that wherever You are, Your Self is Your Eternal companion.

BVII. Ch.4:6-9

6 And even when You have fully accepted the
   belief that there is no past to color the joy and
   peace of the Eternal's gift of Now, time will collapse.
7 In the world, time is an enemy who chases you,
   robbing you of your youth and vitality.
8 The belief in time's past not only prevents You
   from being joy-filled Now, but it also paints a
   bleak and distorted picture of the future.
9 When confronted with the realities of the
   world, the choice between it and the Eternal is
   made without hesitation.

BVII. Ch.5:1-5

I gnoring the responsibility of choosing is not a choice.

2 But know that Love places limits on how much You will be allowed to suffer as a result of believing the wrong ideas about who You are.

3 For Your belief system is solely the result of how You have chosen to interpret the world interpreting You.

4 On the path created for You, You are as You were at the coming forth.

5 One created to be a living recitation of the Beauty and Generosity of the Eternal, One without precedent.

BVII. Ch.5:6-10

6   You are the World Who agreed to find every
    opportunity to express the joy that only comes
    from the Source known as the Eternal.
7   You are the World who agreed to come forth
    in physical form.
8   You agreed to represent a point in consciousness
    of the All That Is; an immense responsibility indeed.
9   Choosing the world in which You believe that
    You can fit into, You make the choice for
    uncertainty.
10 You choose fleeting happiness and a host of
    other maladies that the world asks You to accept,
    but whose effects it knows not how to eradicate.

BVII. Ch.6:1-5

If You think that a real choice exists between the
Eternal and the world, surely there is some hold
which You think the world has over You.

2 Know that no hold is possible over Who is made of
the Eternal, an extension of the Forever.

3 You will attract the witnesses to confirm
whatever belief You hold about Yourself.

4 For that is the power of the Law of Attraction.

5 Choosing the world, many voices will there be
telling You who You are, from where You
come, and how You should conduct Yourself in the
world.

BVII. Ch.6:6-8

6 And because these voices do not host the Will
of the Eternal, the constant changing of their
direction will not only waste Your energy,
but it will also waste You.

7 You will exhaust Yourself going from one fad to
another, the world being incapable of providing
anything of a stable nature.

8 The fatigue of constant disappointment will
only affirm what You already believe about
Yourself (You have no divine origin), when it
could inform You that something in Your life needs
drastic reformation.

BVII. Ch.6:9-11

9 You will plead for relief from the
   circumstances that, by belief and mis-creation,
   You have made.
10 Only to discover that all You need do is
   change Your mind and accept the Eternal's offer
   of admittance into the presence of every good
   thing.
11 Now.

BVII. Ch.7:1-5

Aligning Your awareness with that of the
No-Beginning, No-End is actually what You
agreed to do.

2 Given part of Your Eternity to complete the
journey, You are surely ready to awaken to the
reality of who You are:
3 *You* are scripture; *You* are revelation.
4 *You* are the light of Your way.
5 And through the eons of traveling, through the
compounding of experiences, know that Love
has never abandoned You.

BVII. Ch.7:6-11

6   Love is the Divine substance of which You were created and which, even if You don't know it, You have never lived without, but have often failed to acknowledge.

7   Again, listen as the winds usher in the changing of the seasons.

8   Look at the fading brilliance of the sun as the earth creates distance for the dusk.

9   And if You will but listen carefully, You will hear the prayers of the Worlds.

10 Those brilliant lamps which light and adorn the path of Your return.

11 These are the recitations of Who You are, from where You come, and to where You will inevitably choose to return.

End of Book VII

The Prayer of Continuation

In the Name of the Eternal, the No-Beginning, the No-End. The One who sculpts the Universes and blows the Energy that is Its Divine breath into them. The same Energy that assumes responsibility for the constant flaming of the suns. In the comfort of Love's assurance that You are indeed worthy, and under the protection of the Energy that is Your Divine Inheritance, may Your prayers travel faster than the speed of light. May Your blessings carry with them the power to encourage and inspire the manifestation of every good thing in whomsoever You choose. May Your very thoughts of gratitude for the No-Beginning, No-End create abundance and prosperity that overflows into Your next manifestation if You so choose.

It is in the presence of the Hosts of the Eternal that this prayer is recorded and echoed throughout the Forever.

And it shall come to pass that when You awaken to the Reality of Your Divinity, You will take back this earth and restore it to the heaven that You intended it to be.

Breinigsville, PA USA
27 September 2010
246151BV00006B/1/P